If the sea were sweet...
Seaweed and seashells would
be delicious candy treats.
It sure would be fun, if
the sea were sweet!

Or would it?

Better put on your Thinking
Cap. There may be trouble
up ahead!

SUPPOSE QUE LA MER SOIT SUCRÉE © 1984 by Librairie Larousse, S.A., Paris.
English translation and adaptation by Sandra Beris. © 1984 Larousse & Co., Inc. All rights reserved.
ISBN 0-88332-436-9
Printed in France by Jombart, Évreux.

IF THE SEA WERE SWEET

by Marthe Seguin-Fontes

adapted by Sandra Beris

A THINKING CAP BOOK ™

Larousse & Co. • New York

Imagine how the world would be
If the sea were sweet.

Pebbles would be gumdrops.
Seashells would be a treat.

Seaweed would be candy canes
Or, maybe, lollipops.

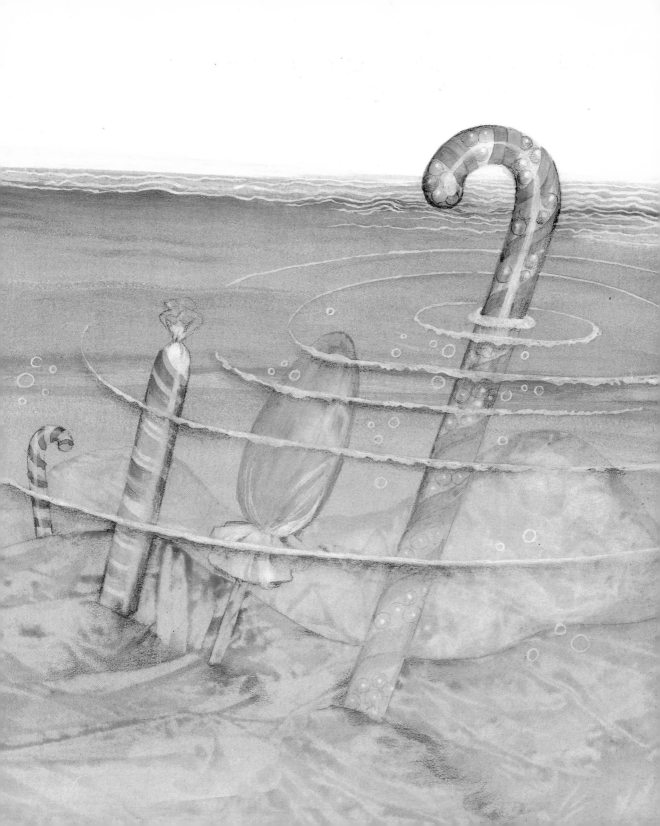

And for an extra special snack
Raspberry fish would hit the spot!

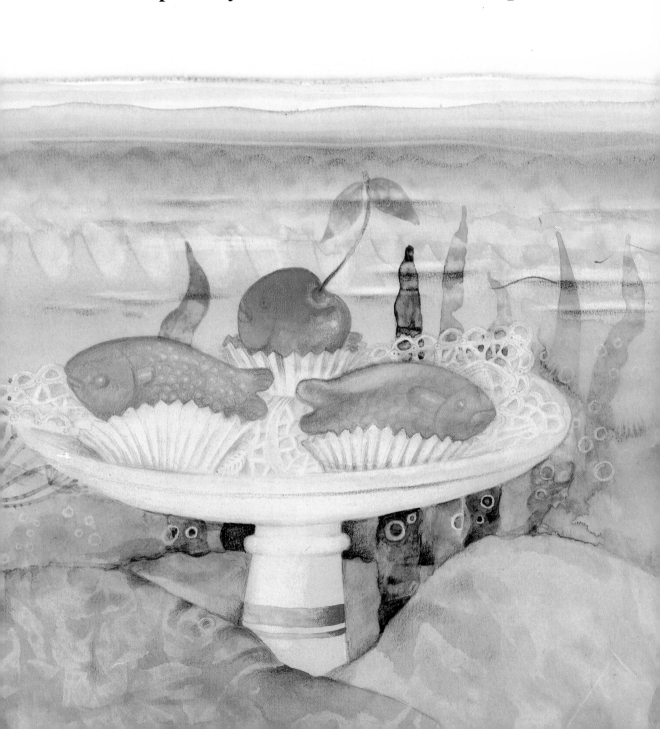

Icebergs would be in demand
Instead of birthday cake.

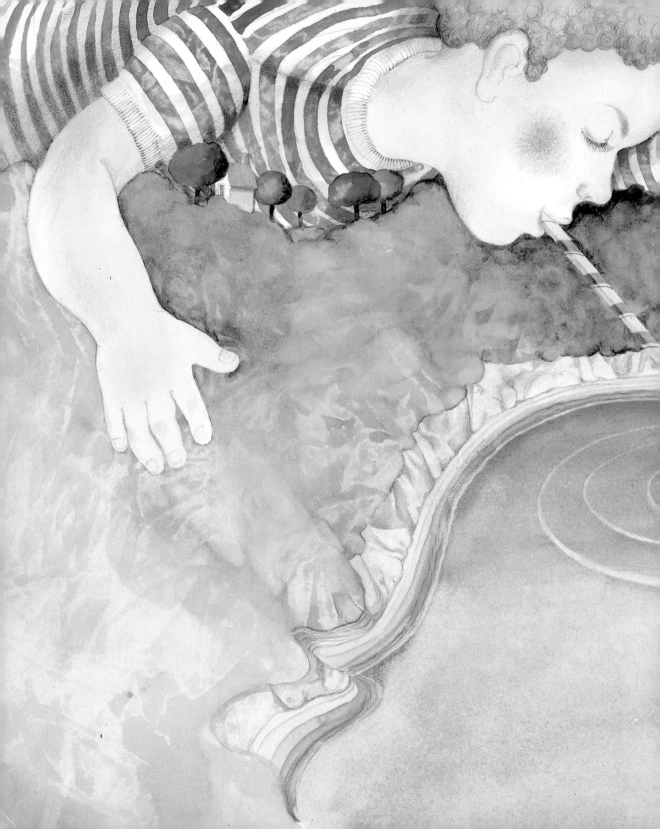

And kids would sip the ocean
Just like a giant shake!

But can you really picture it?
For children love sweets so.
They soon would swallow all the seas.
Yes, every drop would go.

How about the boats then?
Where do you think they'd sail?

And how about sea creatures?
Case in point: the whale.

The whale would look so very sad
Kids would regret what they had done.

They'd have to take each last whale home.
(You know, it might be fun!)

Into a tub each whale would fit.
Then they would feel quite merry.

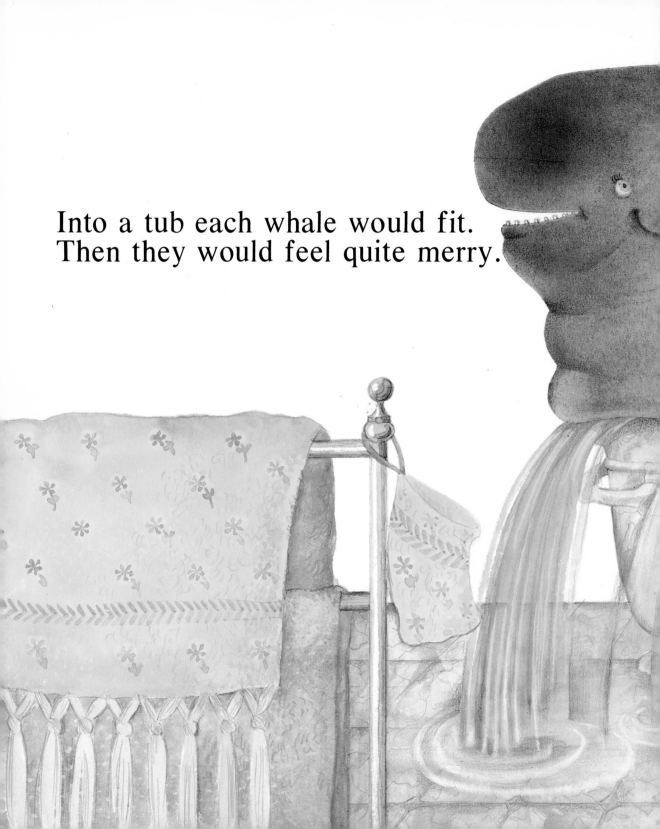

But the neighbors wouldn't like it.
To step out they'd need a ferry!

Because a whale in every bath
Would lead to overflowing
Out windows, doors, and down the street,
Water coming, water going!

Protests! Strikes! Petitions!
Everyone would sign!

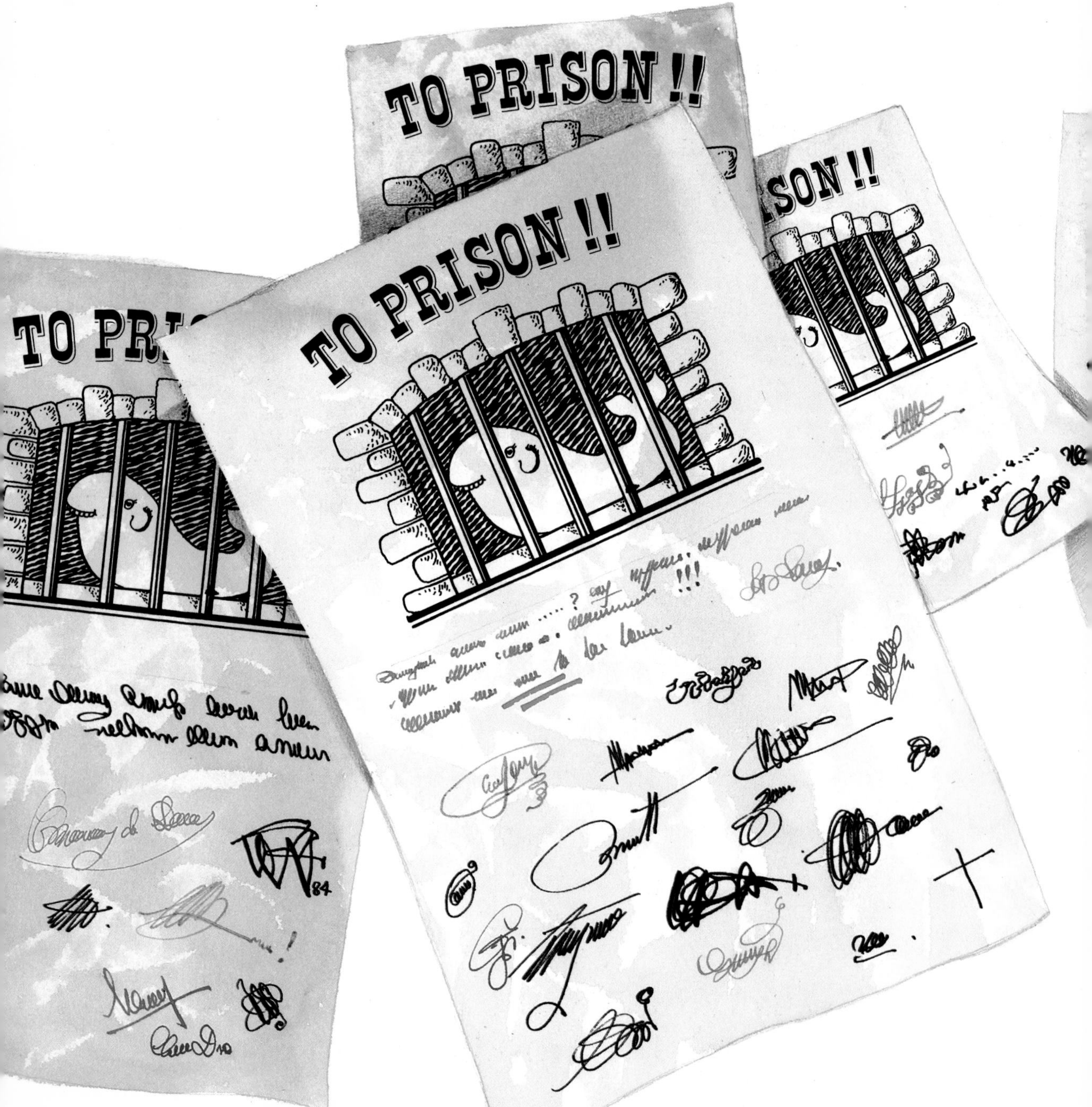
TO PRISON !!
TO PRISON !!
TO PRISON !!

Saying: "Whale keepers off to jail!
Stop the floods in time!"

If you think about the problems
Perhaps it's best for all
That the ocean really isn't sweet.
It's just full of salt!

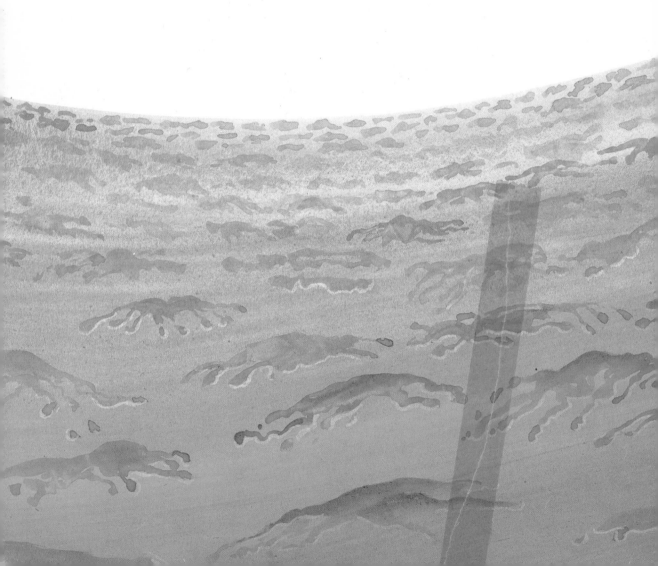